SUPER SHEROES OF HISTORY

Civil

Rights

Women Who Made a Difference

JANEL RODRIGUEZ

Children's Press®
An imprint of Scholastic Inc.

Thank you to Brittany Schulman for her insights into Indigenous Peoples' history and culture.

Picture credits:
Photos ©: cover top: The Granger Collection; cover center top: Jack Corn/The Tennessean/Imagn; cover center bottom: John Dominis/The LIFE Picture Collection/Shutterstock; cover bottom: Bettmann/Getty Images; 5 left: The Granger Collection; 5 center left: Jack Corn/The Tennessean/Imagn; 5 center right: John Dominis/The LIFE Picture Collection/Shutterstock; 5 right: Bettmann/Getty Images; 6 top: Library of Congress; 6 bottom: Chronicle/Alamy Images; 7 top: Glasshouse Images/Alamy Images; 8 bottom: Buyenlarge/Getty Images; 9 top: Charles Moore/Getty Images; 10 top: Cecil Williams/Getty Images; 11 top: Hum Historical/Alamy Images; 11 bottom left: Everett Collection Inc/Alamy Images; 12 top: The Granger Collection; 12 bottom: Rick Lewis/Alamy Images; 13 top: Charles Moore/Getty Images; 14 top: Bettmann/Getty Images; 14 bottom: IanDagnall Computing/Alamy Images; 15 top: The Granger Collection; 15, bottom right: Don Cravens/Getty Images; 16 top: Bettmann/Getty Images; 16 center: Richard Ellis/AFP/Getty Images; 17 top: Mandel Ngan/AFP/Getty Images; 18 top: Carl Iwasaki/Getty Images; 18 bottom: Flip Schulke/Corbis/Getty Images; 19 top: Pictorial Press Ltd/Alamy Images; 20 top: John Dominis/The LIFE Picture Collection/Shutterstock; 20 bottom: The Print Collector/Getty Images; 21 top: Tim Graham/Getty Images; 22 top: Bettmann/Getty Images; 22 bottom: Bob Weston/Getty Images; 23 top: Bettmann/Getty Images; 23 bottom: William J. Smith/AP Images; 24 top: Robert Abbott Sengstacke/Getty Images; 25 top: Frank Empson/The Tennessean/Imagn; 26 top: Horace Cort/AP Images; 26 bottom: Cheryl Chenet/Corbis/Getty Images; 27 center: Everett Collection Inc/Alamy Images; 28 top: Rich Fury/Getty Images; 28 bottom: Universal History Archive/UIG/Shutterstock; 29 top: Buyenlarge/Getty Images; 29 bottom: Universal History Archive/Getty Images; 30 top: AF Archive/Alamy Images; 31 top: Patrick Grehan/Corbis/Getty Images; 31 center: The Granger Collection; 32 top: Paul Christian Gordon/Alamy Images; 32 bottom: Brooks Kraft/Corbis/Getty Images; 33 top: Marc De Simone/Alamy Images; 34 top: Everett Collection/Bridgeman Images; 34 bottom left: Everett Collection Inc/Alamy Images; 35 top left: Bob Parent/Hulton Archive/Getty Images; 36 top: ARCHIVIO GBB/Alamy Images; 37 top: Bettmann/Getty Images; 38 top: Lloyd Wolff/Bridgeman Images; 38 bottom: AP Images; 39 top: Bettmann/Getty Images; 40 top: Jack Corn/The Tennessean/Imagn; 41 top: Saul Loeb/AFP/Getty Images; 41 bottom: Mike Pont/WireImage/Getty Images; 42 top center: Don Cravens/Getty Images; 42 top right: The Granger Collection; 42 bottom left: NAACP/Wikipedia; 42 bottom center: Bob Fitch Photography Archive, Department of Special Collections, Stanford University Library; 43 top right: Carl Juste/Miami Herald/MCT/Sipa USA; 43 bottom left: Bettmann/Getty Images.

All other photos © Shutterstock.

Library of Congress Cataloging-in-Publication Data Available

ISBN 978-1-338-84062-9 (library binding) | ISBN 978-1-338-84063-6 (paperback)

10 9 8 7 6 5 4 3 2 1   23 24 25 26 27

Printed in China   62
First edition, 2023

Series produced for Scholastic by Parcel Yard Press

Contents

Who Are the Super SHEroes of History?

Throughout history, women have ruled countries, led soldiers into battle, changed laws, come up with new ways of thinking, and worked to improve life for everyone. Women's actions and ideas have changed the course of history for whole societies, whole countries, and even the whole world. Women have made a difference. Often, however, their achievements have gone unrecognized.

This book celebrates the life and accomplishments of twelve of these women, twelve Super SHEroes of History! They all fought for equality and civil rights.

Civil rights are the rights that ensure everyone is treated equally. They include the right to vote, the right to education, and the right to use public facilities.

SUPER SHEROES OF HISTORY

Rosa Parks

Diane Nash

Fannie Lou Hamer

Zitkala-Sa

The Super SHEroes in this book held individual protests, organized groups of **activists**, and created political parties. Some worked to improve civil rights for Black Americans, while others focused on rights for Latine people, Indigenous people, or people with disabilities. They gained their reputation through courage, intelligence, and determination. Most of them had to overcome many obstacles in order to achieve their goals, but they were still able to accomplish things that made a difference to the times in which they lived.

This book brings the stories of these Super SHEroes to you! And while you read them, remember:

Your story can make a difference, too. You can become a Super SHEro of History!

Septima Poinsette Clark

After Septima was fired as a schoolteacher for her civil rights activity, she helped to educate an entire generation of Black Americans.

datafile

Born: May 3, 1898

Died: December 15, 1987

Place of birth: Charleston, South Carolina

Role: Educator and activist

Super SHEro for: Teaching thousands of Black Americans their rights as citizens, fueling the civil rights movement

Septima's father, Peter, had been enslaved. Her mother, Victoria, was from Haiti. She had gone to a good school. They both knew the importance of education. They encouraged Septima to learn as much as she could. At age eighteen, Septima qualified as a schoolteacher in her hometown of Charleston, South Carolina.

Charleston, South Carolina ▼

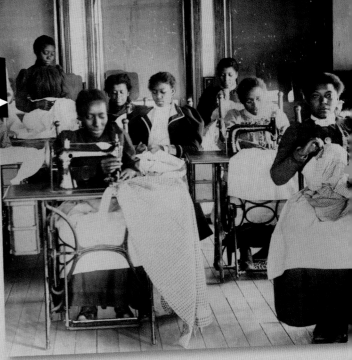

Black students learn sewing in a class at a school in Charleston.

In the 1910s, a **racist** law prevented Black teachers from teaching in public schools in Charleston. It was an example of the **Jim Crow** laws in the South, which kept people of color from having the same rights and **privileges** as white people. Septima found a job on nearby Johns Island.

She also joined the National Association for the Advancement of Colored People (NAACP), an organization that fought **discrimination** against Black people. Septima collected signatures from Black citizens to get the law against Black teachers changed. When the law was dropped in 1920, she took a teaching job in Charleston.

Septima would spend forty years fighting for Black rights, such as getting Black teachers the same pay as white teachers. In the 1950s, the Charleston County School Board grew angry when Septima publicly supported **integration**, or letting Black and white students attend school together. The board made it illegal for teachers to be in civil rights groups like the NAACP, and fired Septima. However, that did not stop her activism.

Public schools in the United States were integrated by law in 1954.

Voter registration classes took place in many locations. This one is in a hairdresser's shop.

Septima already spent her summer vacations running workshops on civil rights at the Highlander Folk School in Tennessee. She taught Black adults how to read and write, and about their rights as US citizens. Septima also showed people how to fill out the forms they needed to complete to register to vote.

When Septima became director of education for the Southern Christian Leadership Conference, a leading civil rights organization, she ran a similar Citizenship Education Program. She founded 800 "citizen education" schools that helped more than one million Black citizens register to vote.

Did You Know?

It was illegal to teach enslaved people to read or write, although white women opposed to slavery often broke the law to teach them anyway. Once slavery ended, southern states tried to keep Black people illiterate. Because citizens had to pass a literacy test before voting, this prevented most Black Americans from exercising their civil rights.

Septima's workshops educated future leaders of the civil rights movement, such as Rosa Parks. After she retired, Septima continued promoting civil rights. In 1972, she won a seat on the Charleston County School Board—the very same board that had fired her sixteen years earlier.

Septima received many awards for her civil rights work before she died in 1987. **Today she is remembered as a Super SHEro whom Martin Luther King, Jr., called "the Mother of the Movement."**

Septima received a special award from Martin Luther King, Jr., for her "service to humanity."

What Would You Do?

Septima lost her well-paying job as a teacher and instead spent much of her career as a volunteer who worked hard for very little pay.

What would make you do a job for little or no pay?

Life in the Times of Septima Poinsette Clark

SOUTH CAROLINA: 1920s

Septima was a child when she first experienced the inequality of **segregation**. Her first school was for Black children only. It had just one teacher for 100 students! Later Septima attended the Avery Normal Institute, where she trained to become a teacher. Forbidden from teaching in Charleston, she found a job on Johns Island, off the coast of South Carolina.

Johns Island was home to poor Black communities.

On the island, Septima saw how great the need was for literacy among Black adults. She saw it as a key to claiming their rights as citizens. She began to teach the adults to read and write—and her life's mission began.

Septima's school on Johns Island taught only Black students.

Rosa Parks

When long-time civil rights activist Rosa Parks refused to give her seat on a bus to a white man, she inspired the overturn of racist laws in the United States.

SUPER
SHEROES
OF HISTORY

As a child in Alabama, Rosa had to walk to school because Black children were not allowed to take the bus. Similar laws were still in place when Rosa married a barber named Raymond Parks and moved to the state capital, Montgomery.

datafile

Born: February 4, 1913

Died: October 24, 2005

Place of birth: Tuskegee, Alabama

Role: Activist

Super SHEro for: Refusing to obey a racist law

CLEVELAND AVE.

The bus where Rosa refused to give up her seat is kept in a museum. ➡

Martin Luther King, Jr., was a young preacher in Montgomery when he became a civil rights leader.

In Montgomery, Rosa joined her husband working with the NAACP. By day Rosa worked as a **seamstress**. By night, she acted as the local NAACP secretary. She wrote letters, went to meetings, and helped arrange protests.

On the evening of December 1, 1955, Rosa left work and got on a bus. She sat in a seat behind the "Whites Only" section.

A few stops later, some white men entered and found all the seats in the front of the bus taken. The bus driver told Rosa and people near her to get up so the white men could sit. (Black and white people were not even allowed to sit next to each other.) Rosa refused. People later said this was because she was tired, but Rosa herself said, "The only tired I was, was tired of giving in."

Rosa re-created her famous bus ride when the laws had been changed.

Did You Know?

Nine months before Rosa was jailed, a Black schoolgirl named Claudette Colvin had also been arrested for refusing to give up a seat on a bus in Montgomery. Claudette's case did not attract the same publicity as Rosa's, however. Rosa's image as a hard-working seamstress made her a better figurehead to lead the protests.

Rosa had her fingerprints taken by police after her arrest.

The bus driver called the police, who arrested Rosa. Rosa's arrest made the newspapers. It inspired the Black community to take action. They decided to **boycott** the buses in Montgomery to protest segregation on public transportation.

For thirteen months, Black people refused to ride on city buses. Finally, on November 13, 1956, the Supreme Court ruled that segregation on buses was not allowed under the US Constitution. It was a great victory for civil rights.

For 381 days during the bus boycott, Black people walked or carpooled to work.

Rosa never stopped working for civil rights for everyone.

Although Rosa spent her time trying to make conditions a little easier for all Black Americans, her activism did not make her own life easy. Both she and her husband were fired from their jobs after her arrest. Once the boycott got underway, she began receiving death threats. After the Supreme Court victory, Rosa and Raymond moved to Detroit, Michigan. There, Rosa worked for the Black congressman John Conyers for over twenty years.

In 1996, President Bill Clinton awarded Rosa the Presidential Medal of Freedom, one of the highest civilian honors in the United States.

Rosa worked for racial equality for the rest of her life, for which she received many awards. There are schools, libraries, museums—and even an asteroid—named for her. When she died in 2005. Rosa's funeral service was attended by 4,000 people. **They hailed her as a Super SHEro who had helped spark the civil rights movement that would end segregation in the United States.**

Rosa became the first woman to lie in the Capitol Rotunda in Washington, DC.

What Would You Do?

Jim Crow laws prevented millions of Black Americans from freely enjoying parks, schools, libraries, restaurants, and stores. It took a lot of courage for people to speak out against this unfair segregation.

Would you be brave enough to stand up for your rights like Rosa, even if it meant going to jail?

ALABAMA: 1950s

Segregation laws were intended to keep Black and white people "separate but equal." Each race had its own facilities, such as schools, churches, and libraries. But the facilities were far from equal.

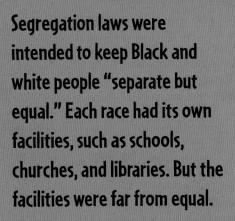

A segregated school in Kansas

WE WANT A WHITE SCHOOL

Young white protestors support segregated schools.

Rosa's elementary school was a single room shared by grades 1 to 6. Meanwhile, white children from the same town attended classes in a brand-new building. Facilities such as restrooms and water fountains for Black citizens were also inferior to those for white people.

Public spaces were divided into marked sections. The front seats of buses and the front tables of restaurants were kept for "whites only." Only white people could use the front doors of buildings. Black people had to enter through the back door.

Marriage between the two races was illegal, as was working together in jobs where they might touch each other, such as nursing or hairdressing.

Protesting these laws, however, meant risking arrest or worse. Some protestors became targets of the Ku Klux Klan (KKK). This group of racial **terrorists** threatened, beat, and killed Black people to stop them from seeking equality.

A water fountain for Black people

Fannie Lou Hamer

SUPER SHEROES OF HISTORY

Fannie Lou was a leading figure in the fight for Black people to have the right to vote. She remains an inspiration for Black women to enter politics.

Fannie Lou was the youngest of twenty children. Her parents were sharecroppers in Mississippi, farmers who gave up part of their crop as rent on their land. It was a hard life. When Fannie Lou was six years old, she began picking cotton with her family. She went to school and learned to read and write a little. But because her family was so poor, she had to leave school at the age of twelve and find a paying job.

datafile

Born: October 6, 1917

Died: March 14, 1977

Place of birth: Ruleville, Mississippi

Role: Activist and speaker

Super SHEro for: Fighting for the right to vote for herself and others

Picking cotton was hard work that had previously often been done by enslaved people.

Plantation homes were usually small and poorly furnished.

When Fannie Lou was twenty-seven, she met and married Perry Hamer. They adopted four daughters and worked on a **plantation** owned by a man named Marlowe. One day in 1962, Fannie Lou attended a meeting held by the Student Nonviolent Coordinating Committee (SNCC). She heard an activist named James Forman speak about how Black people were being beaten or killed for trying to vote. Fannie Lou decided to take a literacy test and register to vote.

Fannie Lou and other activists went to the nearby city of Indianola to take the test. Fannie Lou could read and write, but she failed the test because she could not answer some of the questions. On the way home, the activists were stopped by the police. The police made up a reason to fine them. When Fannie Lou got home, Marlowe fired her.

In 1963, Fannie Lou joined other activists in a **sit-in** protest at a whites-only lunch counter. The activists were arrested, jailed, and beaten by the police. The effect of Fannie Lou's injuries lasted for the rest of her life.

Activists protest segregation in Indianola with a sign reading "Uhuru," an African word meaning "freedom."

The literacy tests took place in the Indianola courthouse.

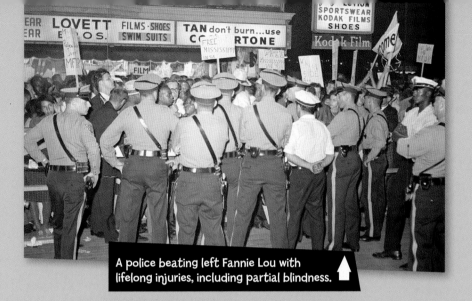

A police beating left Fannie Lou with lifelong injuries, including partial blindness.

Undeterred, Fannie Lou kept taking the voter registration test until she passed. Then, however, she was told that she could only vote if she paid a poll tax. This tax was another obstacle to stop Black people from voting. Fannie Lou decided to create her own political party and set up the Mississippi Freedom Democratic Party. When she voted, she wanted to vote for herself!

Did You Know?

Fannie Lou first learned to make herself heard by singing in church. She had a great voice. She would sing hymns to soothe fellow activists when they were afraid, and would belt out protest songs to incite enthusiasm.

Fannie Lou attended the Democratic National Convention with the parents of an activist who had been murdered.

In 1964, Fannie Lou gave a powerful speech at the Democratic National Convention about the racism Black people met when they tried to vote. "Is this America?" Fannie Lou asked. "The land of the free and home of the brave?" Fannie Lou's speech helped the Voting Rights Act of 1965 to get passed. The act banned race-based restrictions on voting, such as literacy tests and poll taxes.

NEVER GIVE UP!

STOP RACISM

FREEDOM TO VOTE

Later in her career, Fannie Lou encouraged women to enter politics and run for office. She also launched programs to help Black Americans own land and grow crops and to create a "pig bank" to supply fresh pork to poor families. The programs were expensive, however, and closed after a few years.

Fannie Lou died in 1977. **On her tombstone are famous words from one of her speeches: "I'm sick and tired of being sick and tired."**

People called Fannie Lou "illiterate" because of her southern way of expressing herself, but she was a powerful public speaker.

What Would You Do?

Because she tried to vote, Fannie Lou lost her job and her home, got beaten up, and was made to take unfair tests and pay unfair taxes.

If you experienced these obstacles, would you keep trying to vote or give up?

Why is it so important to be able to vote?

Life in the Times of Fannie Lou Hamer
MISSISSIPPI: 1964

Resistance to allowing Black people to vote was strong in Mississippi. Literacy tests and police mistreatment prevented Black people from registering to vote. Fannie Lou experienced it herself. To fight for voting rights, she helped organize Freedom Summer.

Activists register Black Americans to vote.

A Black woman votes in an election in Mississippi.

This civil rights campaign recruited college students from the North, who were mainly white, to help Black people in Mississippi register to vote. About 1,000 young people volunteered.

The volunteers were trained in teaching citizenship classes and in filling out registration forms.

They were also warned to expect trouble. Volunteers were told to bring money in case they were arrested and needed to post **bail** to get themselves released.

A week into the program, a Black church in Mississippi was set on fire. Three volunteers who went to investigate were later found murdered by the Ku Klux Klan.

Freedom Summer carried on, but it was not a big success. Of the 17,000 Black residents who attempted to register to vote, only 1,600 succeeded.

Martin Luther King, Jr., holds pictures of the murdered volunteers.

Dolores Huerta

Dolores Huerta worked to improve farmworkers' rights. She started a **union** to work for better pay and conditions for workers, who were mainly migrants from Mexico and other parts of Latin America.

SUPER SHEROES OF HISTORY

Dolores was born in New Mexico.
She moved to California with her mother when she was three, after her parents divorced. Her mother taught her that she had an obligation to help people who needed assistance. She also told Dolores to take action, rather than waiting for people to ask for help.

Latine farmworkers often lived in poor conditions.

datafile

Born: April 10, 1930

Place of birth: Dawson, New Mexico

Role: Organizer and activist

Super SHEro for: Helping the Latine community stand up for their rights with a "Sí, se puede!" ("Yes, we can!") attitude

Dolores's father was a state politician. From him, Dolores inherited a skill for organization and politics. A former coal miner, he supported unions as a way for workers to secure fair pay, benefits, and working conditions.

Dolores became a teacher in the Central Valley of California. Many of her students were from different Spanish-speaking backgrounds, but they had one thing in common: poverty. Their parents worked on farms under terrible conditions. The sight of hungry children made Dolores decide to take action.

Many of the farmworkers in California came from Mexico.

Mexican farmworkers ride to the fields on a truck.

Dolores campaigned to persuade farmworkers to join the union.

Dolores volunteered at the Community Service Organization (CSO), which campaigned to improve the lives of Latine workers in California. She helped pass state laws to improve their conditions. A few years later she met César Chávez, and together they left the CSO to start a union for farmworkers. It later became known as the United Farm Workers.

In 1965, Dolores and Chávez organized a **strike** of grape pickers in Delano, California. The grape pickers wanted a pay raise, but the employers refused.

Dolores and her supporters urged people not to buy any products made with grapes. Protests spread around the country. In five years, 17 million Americans stopped eating grapes. The boycott finally forced grape growers to agree to give the workers better pay and conditions. It was a historic win.

Farmworkers vote in a meeting about a strike.

Dolores appears at a press conference about the grape pickers' strike.

Dolores scored other wins for farmworkers, too. She successfully campaigned for families with young children to get financial support from the US government. She also got them disability insurance, so if they got hurt on the job and could not work, they could still get paid.

Marchers carry a giant puppet of Dolores in a march for women's rights in 2017.

Dolores believed the best way to help others was to teach them to help themselves, saying, "You have the power within you." Her most famous slogan came about when she answered farmworkers who did not believe they could win their battles. "We can't do it," they'd say in Spanish, "No se puede." "Sí, se puede," Dolores would reply. "Yes, we can!"

Did You Know?

In 2012, President Barack Obama awarded Dolores the Presidential Medal of Freedom, one of the highest honors a civilian can receive in the United States. He thanked her for "letting" him "steal" her slogan, "Yes, we can!" when he ran for president.

When Dolores was fifty-eight years old, she was at a protest where she and other demonstrators were beaten by the police. She was taken to the hospital with serious injuries and took a long time to recover.

Dolores became an **advocate** for women's rights, especially encouraging Latinas to enter politics. She also founded the Dolores Huerta Foundation. She is still fighting for civil rights in her nineties. **She says, "La lucha sigue"—"The fight continues."**

Dolores began the Dolores Huerta Foundation to continue her campaign for civil rights.

What Would You Do?

When Dolores was a teacher, she saw that her students and their families were poor and hungry. She decided to help them.

If you were a teacher and knew your students were living in terrible conditions, how might you help them?

Life in the Times of Dolores Huerta

CALIFORNIA: 1950s & 1960s

In the 1950s and 1960s, most farmworkers in California came from Spanish-speaking countries. A special program allowed them to come to the United States to help with the harvest, but they did not have the same rights as US citizens.

Workers pull up carrots in California.

If workers spoke up against their conditions, they risked being fired or even **deported**. Fruit and vegetable growers took advantage of this. They paid workers about a dollar an hour for long days of backbreaking work under the sun. When workers got thirsty, they had to pay for drinking water.

DISARM THE RICH FARMER on ARM THE WORKER FOR SELF-DEFENSE

B 16 14

Mexican–American farmworkers on strike

César Chávez leads a protest for improved conditions for lettuce pickers.

There were no bathrooms available in the fields, either. If workers got too sick to work, they did not get paid. They did not receive health insurance, so they could not afford medical care.

When Dolores visited farmworkers in their homes near the fields, she found them living in shacks with dirt floors. The conditions reminded her of how enslaved people had lived one hundred years earlier.

Dolores believed the answer was to unionize the workers. By acting together, the workers could persuade the growers to improve their pay and conditions. That was why Dolores and César started what became the United Farm Workers.

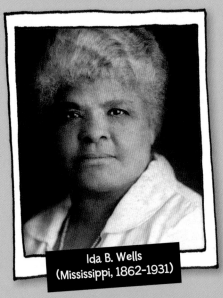

Civil
Rights
JOURNALISM

Ida B. Wells
(Mississippi, 1862-1931)

Ida B. Wells

Ida was born to enslaved parents just before slavery was officially abolished in the United States. She grew up to be a teacher. When she was removed from a first-class train car for being Black in 1884, she wrote an article about it. She decided to become a journalist. Ida wrote about the **lynching** of Black people in the South. She was one of the first people to bring these **atrocities** to national attention.

Ida's life was threatened and she moved to Chicago. There she fought for equal rights for both Black people and women. She helped start the NAACP in 1909, championed women's **suffrage**, and even ran for senator for Illinois!

Zitkala-Sa

Zitkala-Sa was born on the Yankton Sioux **reservation** in South Dakota. When she was eight years old, she was forced to attend a special boarding school for Indigenous children, where she had to cut her hair and change her name to Gertrude. She later went to college and became a musician. When she visited the reservation as a young woman, she found that white settlers were stealing the land. She worried that white settlement was erasing the Sioux way of life. She gave herself a new Sioux name, Zitkala-Sa, and began writing about tribal culture. In 1926, she helped form the National Council of American Indians and fought for Indigenous people's civil rights. Her writings continue to influence important public policies today.

Zitkala-Sa (Gertrude Simmons Bonnin)
(South Dakota, 1876-1938)

Dorothy Height

Dorothy was a social worker who later led civil rights programs at the National Council of Negro Women, an important civil rights organization where she was president for forty years. She campaigned for many causes, including ending lynching. Dorothy advised presidents and first ladies on civil rights issues, and she helped organize the March on Washington for Jobs and Freedom in 1963.

Dorothy Height
(Virginia, 1912-2010)

Shirley Chisholm

Shirley Chisholm
(New York, 1924-2005)

Shirley entered politics to help poor families in Brooklyn. She was the first Black woman elected to Congress (1968). She worked on causes such as food programs for the poor. She was the first female Black candidate for a major political party to run for president of the United States, and was an inspiration to other women of color to enter politics.

Patsy Mink

Patsy Mink
(Hawaii, 1927–2002)

A Japanese American from Hawaii, Patsy was the first woman of color elected to Congress, in 1964. After all her medical school applications were rejected because she was female, Patsy was determined to fight against discrimination. She became a lawyer before going into politics.

In Congress, Patsy's greatest achievement was passing Title IX. This law made it illegal to exclude women from government-funded educational programs, such as sports. Since then, female participation in high school sports has increased over 900 percent. When Patsy died, Title IX was renamed the Patsy Mink Equal Opportunity in Education Act in her honor.

Diane Nash
(Chicago, born 1938)

Civil **Rights** ACTIVISM

Diane Nash

As a college student living in Tennessee, Diane took classes on how to conduct nonviolent protests. She soon began to organize sit-ins and marches against segregation. She once confronted the mayor of Nashville in public and forced him to admit that segregation was wrong.

Diane helped found the Student Nonviolent Coordinating Committee (SNCC) to organize youth protests throughout the country. She persuaded white women to sit with Black people at lunch counters to protest their segregation. She later worked with Dr. Martin Luther King, Jr., on the voting rights campaign that led to the 1965 Voting Rights Act. This act made it illegal to prevent people from voting because of their race or color.

Civil
Rights
ACTIVISM

Myrlie Evers-Williams

After her activist husband, Medgar, was murdered by the Ku Klux Klan, Myrlie became a national speaker, wrote books, and earned a college degree. She was appointed to leadership roles in the Democratic Party, the LA Board of Public Works, and the NAACP in California. She now chairs an institute named after her and Medgar.

Dr. Myrlie Evers-Williams
(Mississippi, born 1933)

Chai Feldblum
(New York, born 1959)

Chai Feldblum

Chai is a lawyer who worked for the Equal Opportunity Employment Commission under President Obama. She helped write the Americans with Disabilities Act of 1990, which helps the disabled access the same job opportunities, schools, and public transportation enjoyed by others. She continues to promote rights for the disabled as vice-chair of the AbilityOne Commission.

Civil
Rights
POLITICS

41

SUPER SHEROES OF HISTORY

Timeline
Here are some highlights in the lives of civil rights Super SHEroes.

Zitkala-Sa helps found the National Council of American Indians.

The Montgomery Bus Boycott ends after 381 days with the desegregation of federal buses.

Diane Nash helps found the Student Nonviolent Coordinating Committee, which encourages young adults to protest segregation peacefully.

| 1909 | 1926 | 1955 | 1956 | 1957 | 1960 | 1962 |

Ida B. Wells helps form the National Association for the Advancement of Colored People (NAACP).

Rosa Parks refuses to give up her seat on a bus in Montgomery, Alabama, sparking the modern civil rights movement.

Septima Clark starts teaching citizenship classes. She inspires the creation of more than 800 "citizenship schools."

Dolores Huerta, along with César Chávez, creates the first union for farm laborers, the National Farm Worker Association (later United Farm Workers).

NAACP
FOUNDED
1909

NATIONAL ASSOCIATION FOR THE ADVANCEMENT OF COLORED PEOPLE

Dorothy Height helps arrange the March on Washington, a historic civil rights protest in which more than 250,000 people take part.

The Voting Rights Act makes it illegal to prevent Black Americans, or citizens of any race, from voting in elections.

Patsy Mink helps draft the Equal Educational Opportunities Act (Title IX), allowing girls equal access to government-funded sports programs.

Kamala Harris is the first female, and the first woman of color, to become vice president of the United States.

| 1963 | 1964 | 1965 | 1968 | 1972 | 1990 | 2021 |

The Civil Rights Act ends segregation by making discrimination based on race, color, age, religion, nationality, and gender illegal.

Shirley Chisholm becomes the first Black woman elected to Congress.

Chai Feldblum helps write and pass the Americans with Disabilities Act, protecting the disabled from discrimination in the workplace.

Fannie Lou Hamer delivers a powerful speech at the Democratic National Convention describing the violence suffered by Black Americans trying to vote in the South.

SUPER SHEROES OF HISTORY

Where in the World?

1. Shirley Chisholm
New York City
Shirley was elected as a congresswoman to represent New York State's 11th congressional district in New York City.

2. Septima Clark
Charleston, South Carolina
Septima was fired as a teacher in Charleston for her civil rights work. She was eventually elected to the same school board that fired her.

3. Myrlie Evers-Williams
Jackson, Mississippi
Myrlie started an institute in Jackson to continue her husband's work for civil rights through education for young people.

4. Chai Feldblum
Washington, DC
Chai's law practice in Washington, DC, focuses on working to influence the passing of new laws, particularly around issues concerning disabilities in the workplace.

5. Fannie Lou Hamer
Winona, Mississippi
Fannie Lou was beaten in jail after a sit-in protest in Winona. She later helped organize Freedom Summer in Mississippi.

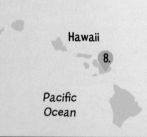

Pacific Ocean

7.

Hawaii
8.

Pacific Ocean

6. Dorothy Height
Washington, DC
Dorothy helped arrange the March on Washington in 1963. Around 250,000 people marched for jobs and freedom.

7. Dolores Huerta
Central Valley, California

After witnessing the working conditions of farm laborers in California's Central Valley, Dolores helped create the United Farm Workers to protect their rights.

9. Diane Nash
Nashville, Tennessee

Diane organized peaceful public protests as a student in Nashville before coordinating youth action around the country.

10. Rosa Parks
Montgomery, Alabama

Rosa refused to give up her seat on a bus and inspired the thirteenth-month-long Montgomery Bus Boycott.

11. Ida B. Wells
Memphis, Tennessee

After Ida started to write about lynching, she received so many threats she had to leave Memphis for her own safety.

12. Zitkala-Sa
Yankton Indian Reservation, South Dakota

Zitkala-Sa was born on a Sioux Indian Reservation in South Dakota, but she later moved to Washington, DC.

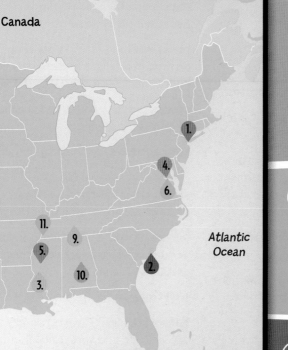

Canada

12.

1.

4.

6.

11.

9.

5.

10.

3.

2.

Atlantic Ocean

Mexico

8. Patsy Mink
Hawaii

After studying law, Patsy could not find a job, so she ran for Hawaii's House of Representatives in 1956. She was elected to the US Congress in 1964.

Glossary

activists (**ak**-tuh-vists) people who support a cause and believe in taking action to change things

advocate (**ad**-vuh-kit) a person who supports an idea or plan

atrocities (uh-**traw**-suh-teez) very cruel or terrible crimes against people

bail (bayl) money paid to a court for the release of someone accused of a crime

boycott (**boi**-kaht) a refusal to do business as a punishment or protest

deported (di-**por**-tuhd) sent back to one's country of origin

discrimination (dis-*krim*-i-**nay**-shuhn) prejudice or unfair trearment to others based on differences in such things as age, race, or gender

illiterate (i-**lit**-ur-it) being unable to read or write

integration (*in*-ti-**gray**-shuhn) the act of making facilities open to people of all races and ethnic groups

Jim Crow (jim kroh) a name given to laws passed by southern states to make segregation legal

literacy (**lit**-ur-uh-see) the ability to read and write

lynching (**lin**-ching) a sometimes public murder by a group of people, often involving hanging

plantation (plan-**tay**-shuhn) a large farm where crops such as coffee, rubber, and cotton are grown

privileges (**priv**-uh-lij-*uz*) special rights or advantages given to a person or a group of people

racist (**ray**-sist) treating someone unfairly or cruelly because of their race

reservation (rez-ur-**vay**-shuhn) an area of land set aside by the government for a special purpose

seamstress (**seem**-stris) a woman who sews for a living

segregation (*seg*-ri-**gay**-shuhn) the act of keeping people or groups apart

sit-in (sit in) the occupation of a place or facility as a form of protest

strike (strike) a situation in which workers refuse to work until their demands are met

suffrage (**suhf**-rij) the right to vote

terrorists (**ter**-ur-ists) people who use violence and threats to frighten people or obtain power

union (**yoon**-yuhn) an organized group of workers set up to help improve such things as working conditions, wages, and health benefits

Index

Further Reading

Dionne, Evette. *Lifting As We Climb: Black Women's Battle for the Ballot Box*. New York: Viking, 2020.

London, Martha. *Claudette Colvin (Amazing Young People)*. Minneapolis, Minn: Pop!, 2019.

Sjonger, Rebecca. *Ida B. Wells: Lynching, Our National Crime (Deconstructing Powerful Speeches)*. New York: Crabtree Publishing Company, 2021.

Yomtov, Nel. *The Movement: 1955 (Exploring Civil Rights)*. New York: Scholastic, 2022.

About the Author

Janel Rodriguez is a "Nuyorican"—that is, a Puerto Rican born and raised in New York City. Her family, like most Puerto Ricans today, descends from a mix of Native American, Black, and white ancestors. Although their skin tones may differ, they all share one thing in common: the same rights and privileges as other Americans. This is thanks to the work of civil rights activists like those featured in this book.

Janel has previously written books and articles about Latina and Black American SHEroes and enjoys writing children's fiction, too. When she isn't tapping away on her laptop, she can be found making art—especially drawing or painting portraits of people (including some of SHEroes!).

About the Consultant

Bonnie Morris grew up in California, North Carolina, and Washington, DC. She earned her PhD in women's history and is the author of nineteen books, including *Women's History For Beginners*, *The Feminist Revolution*, and *What's the Score? 25 Years of Teaching Women's Sports History*. She is also a scholarly adviser to the National Women's History Museum and a historical consultant to Disney Animation. In one of her favorite jobs as a professor, she lived on a ship and went around the world (three times!) teaching for Semester at Sea. She has kept a journal since she was twelve and has filled more than 200 notebooks using a fountain pen.